Mennonite Statements on Peace 1915–1966

A Historical and Theological Review of
Anabaptist-Mennonite Concepts of
Peace Witness and Church-State Relations

By Richard C. Detweiler

WIPF & STOCK · Eugene, Oregon

Wipf and Stock Publishers
199 W 8th Ave, Suite 3
Eugene, OR 97401

Mennonite Statements on Peace 1915-1966
A Historical and Theological Review of Anabaptist-Mennonite
Concepts of Peace Witness and Church-State Relations
By Detweiler, Richard C.
Copyright © 1968 Herald Press All rights reserved.
Softcover ISBN-13: 978-1-5326-9431-8
Hardcover ISBN-13: 978-1-5326-9432-5
Publication date 6/11/2020
Previously published by Herald Press, 1968

Preface

Heretofore I have not explored with sufficiently serious critical intent the area of church and state relations. I will need to let your judgment determine whether this presentation contributes anything toward clarification of Mennonite Church peace witness developments from 1915 to 1966.

This booklet attempts first to review the main aspects of the early Anabaptist-Mennonite position on church and state. I have drawn largely from the Anabaptist-Mennonite research of competent scholars. Some translated primary sources were also used. Second, I have attempted to evaluate the peace witness documents representing the Mennonite Church during 1915-66. These documents were supplied by the Committee on Peace and Social Concerns. Included was a summary of the peace witness of the Mennonite Church (through the CPSC and its predecessors) to other Christians, to the state, and to society, with respect to peace and the social implications of the gospel (1915-66), prepared by Guy F. Hershberger, December 1, 1966. I had access also to statements of criticism directed toward the work of the Mennonite Church peace committees. The examination of peace witness documents is directed particularly toward bringing into view changes and trends within the period, 1915-66.

Third, some theological implications of Mennonite Church peace witness trends are developed, both in relation to historic Anabaptist-Mennonite understandings and also in the light of contemporary developments as reflected in current concepts of the state in contemporary theological thought. Fourth, an attempt is made to bring the findings of this study to a focus, with a view to facilitate progress toward a brotherhood consensus that is necessary to undergird our mission of peace witness.

Several limitations of this study must be frankly recognized.

1. The theological features and trends of Mennonite peace witness are inseparable from historical contexts. Our inadequacies of information and understanding of the dynamics operating in a given historical setting may qualify the accuracy of our interpretations.

2. Official church documents may not always reveal underlying trends, since such documents are generally formulated on end-points of agreement. Changing positions are often first and more observable in group

4

discussions, personal correspondence to and from church leaders involved in peace witness, studies preliminary to the preparation of documents, sermons and articles preached and written unofficially for church consumption, and the life-forms of peace witness in which members of the brotherhood engage.

3. It is difficult to discern to what extent the representations of church peace witness reflect brotherhood consensus, since responsible peace agencies may have no clear way of knowing, except through discussion and adoption. Furthermore, it is expected that a church peace agency should assert prophetic leadership which at times may result in creative tension which is preliminary and necessary to arriving at valid consensus and position.

4. The categories employed for a theological discussion of Mennonite peace witness have a bearing upon the direction the discussion takes, although they do not presuppose the conclusions reached. However, the categories for any evaluation must be chosen and do *make a difference*.

5. I have not entered into primary biblical exegesis in detail with regard to the New Testament passages relevant to the subject, but I have tried to do sufficient "homework" in my study so that the examinations made and presented are informed by New Testament concepts.

This study was made an individual reading course approved for incorporation into a ThM program at Princeton Theological Seminary. I submitted the outline of approach and bibliography to the supervisor of the course, Dr. M. Richard Shaull. The study, therefore, is an independent one, although related to seminary course work. It was done in a relatively brief period of time and does not reflect the benefit of prolonged seasoning. A more coherent wholeness and desired conciseness may have resulted from a more gradual assimilation of material.

Contents

A Review of Early Anabaptist-Mennonite Views of Church and State

Doctrine of the Church

Before we examine the sixteenth-century Anabaptist view of the state, we need to look at the Anabaptist concept of the church which was a voluntary and exclusive fellowship of believers in Jesus Christ, committed to follow Him in full obedience as Lord. The church, according to the Anabaptist, is a *Gemeinde*, a community or brotherhood, not primarily an institution, although not without structure.

Since the church is a called-out body separated from the "world," it has a redeemed nature. The church is both "other-worldly" in character and at the same time takes form in the world. The life and function of the church and the state (which is part of the "world") involve two different realities. That which pertains to life in one is not proper to the other although the two are related.

"The Anabaptist Vision was not a detailed blueprint for the reconstruction of human society, but

9

the Brethren did believe that Jesus intended that the kingdom of God should be set up in the midst of the earth, here and now, and this they proposed to do forthwith." [1]

The Theology of Discipleship

The well-known view of Harold S. Bender is that the Anabaptist conception of the church is ultimately derivative from its concept of Christianity as discipleship. Others would give priority to the Anabaptist concern for the restitution of the true church (Franklin H. Littell), or the authority of the Scriptures (Donovan Smucker), or the doctrine of the two worlds (Robert Friedmann). It is certainly true, however, that the "following Christ" motif constitutes a substantial element of Anabaptist "theology," and comes into play strongly as the predominant determinative for Anabaptist relations with the "world" including civil government.

The Authority of the Scriptures

An understanding of the Anabaptist view of the relation of church and state must take into account the utter seriousness with which Anabaptists seek to obey the authority of the Scriptures above any expediencies or compromises in their contemporary situation. The main principles guiding Anabaptist biblical interpretation are: (1) The Word, intent, and Spirit of Christ, [2] (2) the finality of the New Testament in all matters of doctrine and practice, and (3)

10

the dynamic interrelation of Scripture, Spirit, and brotherhood in discerning the will of God.

An Overview of Church and State

Up to the time of Hans J. Hillerbrand's doctoral dissertation (1957)[3] a thoroughgoing and comprehensive analysis of the Anabaptist view of the state was not available. Hillerbrand's basic conclusions seemingly support positions generally held earlier by scholars in the Anabaptist-Mennonite tradition (such as John Horsch, Harold S. Bender, Guy F. Hershberger, and J. C. Wenger), and for the most part have been accepted as definitive of sixteenth-century Anabaptist views. Bender, for example, in the first half of his article in *The Mennonite Encyclopedia* on the "Anabaptist-Mennonite Attitude Toward the State" (Vol. IV, pp. 611-19), follows Hillerbrand's dissertation summary almost word for word.

Hillerbrand concludes from the evidence at hand that the sixteenth-century Anabaptist position with regard to the state is the deliberate outcome of a thorough, systematic, and basically consistent understanding of the Scriptures. He holds that it is not the by-product of a biblical naiveté which is not aware of the complexities of social life or which seeks to justify a position that has to be taken in any case by force of circumstances. That is not to say that *all* Anabaptists fully comprehended what we now call the Anabaptist concept, but the same was true also

11

of persons related to other Reformation streams of thought.

Three points of broad significance may be seen in the Anabaptist view of the state. (1) The *corpus Christianum* concept is absolutely rejected. Anabaptists insist that church and state are essentially and functionally two distinctly separate orders and cannot be "numerically identical" or compose one unified order. (2) The particular understanding of the Scriptures that underlies the Anabaptist view of the Christian and state relations is that the coming of Christ has brought about a new situation. Therefore the relation of God to governmental authority and the Christian's relation to civil government are now under the New Testament ethic which supersedes that of the Old Testament. (3) The Anabaptists see a dualism between the kingdom of Christ and the "world." The true church of voluntary believers expresses the visible form of redeemed life under the rule of Christ. The "world" is the kingdom of darkness characterized by demonic powers, the realm in which the state must function "outside the perfection of Christ."

The Nature of the State

Anabaptist writers affirm that the office of government is ordained by God as a necessary provision for the ordering of human society, because of the disorder resulting from human sin. Consequently, Anabaptists view the ordering of society by God through the state as expressing both the wrath and the grace of God, a view essentially held by all the Reformers.

A qualitative distinction between good and bad government is not made. The necessity of civil order is consistently upheld. Rebellion against the state is excluded as a rightful option, regardless of how evil a given state may be in its performance. The state is viewed from the standpoint of the necessity of its "sword-character" or coercive power to maintain order.

Functions and Limitations of the State

It follows from the nature of the state that its main function is the ordering of human society. Specifically, its tasks are to punish evildoers and to protect law-abiding citizens, although its "welfare service" is far from unknown to early Anabaptists. Pilgram Marpeck's civil engineering employment is an example.

Governmental authorities are deemed the "servants of God." As such they are to consider themselves not absolute in power but subject to God. At this point, Hillerbrand's judgment that the power and authority of government, in Anabaptist thinking, includes the right over life and death of its people, [4] must be qualified by the positions of Anabaptist leaders who not only deny the right of capital punishment to Christians serving in government, but who also protest the use of governmental office for

13

dealing the death penalty. [5] Rulers are not to exercise jurisdiction over the consciences and faith of others. While Anabaptists consistently affirm their willingness to obey civil government in "temporal" matters, they see the realm of faith as under the dominion of Christ. When the state extends its authority to this realm, it is usurping power beyond its ordained function and may rightfully be disobeyed.

Hillerbrand summarizes the basic reasons for Anabaptist willingness to obey governmental authority: [6]

1. Obedience to the state is one aspect of the more general obedience to God who has ordained government.

2. The basis of such obedience is the command of Scripture and the example of Jesus.

3. Obedience to temporal authority is independent of the moral character of a given state since Christian obedience is motivated not by fear of punishment but by the desire to fulfill the will of God.

4. The limits of Anabaptist obedience are related to their understanding that the legitimate functions of any government embrace only the exercise of public law and order and do not include jurisdiction over the spiritual realm.

5. For Anabaptists, the limits of obedience are to be expressed in passive refusal, not in active rebellion or revolution against the existing order. This point distinguishes mainline evangelical Anabaptism from its extreme aberrations.

In addition to appropriate submission and obedience, the obligations to the state generally accepted as Christian duty are intercessory prayer for rulers, the payment of taxes (with some exceptions to the payment of war taxes and "hangman's dues"), and the rendering of honor and respect to governing authorities, since all these are grounded specifically in New Testament injunctions.

Participation in Government

Although men such as Conrad Grebel, Felix Manz, Pilgram Marpeck, and others had the necessary prerequisites to hold government office, the Anabaptists by and large concluded [7] that a Christian could not occupy a governmental office since the principles underlying the office of government are of a coercive nature and basically incompatible with the principles of the gospel imperative for every Christian.

This view constitutes a major difference between Anabaptists and the Reformers who see state office-holding as a Christian vocation. Anabaptists spell out their rejection of participation in government (particularly thought of as the "magistracy") with four major reasons: [8]

1. The example of Christ Himself speaks against it.

2. There is in the Scriptures no evidence for such participation by a true Christian. (Such examples as Cornelius the centurion, Acts 10, are considered inconclusive since post-conversion details are not given).

3. The teachings of Christ show an incompatibility between the worldly principles of lordship and might in government rule and the suffering-servant posture of the

Christian. Matthew 20:25-27.

4. A radical church-world distinction means the Christian is solely concerned with following Christ and does not have responsibilities for maintaining law and order in the world.

Participation in War

Absolute nonresistance is the most clear-cut way in which the position of Anabaptism with respect to the state is expressed. It is not necessary to repeat here the documented evidence for this position. The basis is the example and command of Christ which constitute the supreme ethic for true Christian disciples.

Therefore, as Conrad Grebel says: "Neither do they [true Christian believers] use worldly sword or war, since all killing has ceased with them—unless, indeed, we are still of the old law." [9] Implicit in this view is the stance of church and state separation since the Anabaptists speak primarily, though not exclusively, of the *Christian* in relation to war and do not clarify their view as to whether the state can rightfully engage in armed conflict.

Peter Riedemann, the Hutterian leader, wrote in 1545: "Christ the Prince of Peace, has established His kingdom, that is, His church, and has purchased it by His blood. In this kingdom all worldly warfare has ended. Therefore, a Christian has no part in war nor does he wield the sword to execute vengeance." [10]

The Anabaptist attitude is primarily "defenseless-

16

ness" and not "pacifism."[11] The emphasis is on suffering by members of Christ's kingdom for His sake rather than on the hope of bringing in a general ordering of society in which coercion would be unnecessary. The social order is viewed pessimistically and cannot be "Christianized."

Witness to Governmental Authorities

Since the civil rulers of sixteenth-century European states claim to be Christians, Anabaptist witness to the state is oriented toward reminding the authorities of their Christian duty. This witness at the same time generally denies the Christian character of governmental authorities and even more basically denies that a true Christian could conscientiously participate in the functions of governmental office, at least those of a directly coercive nature.

It is difficult to ascertain what difference there might have been in the attitude and substance of the witness of Anabaptists to an avowedly secular government since their exhortation and admonition were generally directed in part to denunciation of state-church religion and to the ungodly actions of professing Christians in power. Also, Anabaptist confrontation with civil officials most often occurred under pressure circumstances which involved some measure of verbal self-defense. Thus it is difficult to presume what the Anabaptist witness might have been in a free society.

Sixteenth-century Anabaptist-Mennonite witness did remind the civil authorities of their governmental duties beyond the motive of the Anabaptists' self-preservation or privilege. Before the Waldshut Town Council, Claus Felbinger says:

"God has given the sword into your hand. He has granted you such honor and dignity as is meet, that you may be rightly obeyed in that which is not against God. And we say to you: 'He who withstands the authorities in just matters withstands God's ordinance, for the authorities hold their office in order that disobedience might be punished. This is the reason, you servants of God, that I wanted to remind and exhort you to consider your office, not that we were dismayed at having to suffer for what we have done for the sake of our confession. Oh, no!' "[12]

Because of the *corpus Christianum* concept under which the medieval European society was structured, the Anabaptist witness to governmental authorites, to other Christians, and to society at large (all of which were considered "Christian") was of one piece. To witness to one was to witness to all.

Furthermore, the Anabaptist witness is not directed to the state as a kind of nonpersonal entity, but to men in power, with an apparent view to their conversion to obedience to the Word of Christ and a consequent change of ethic and rejection of the magistracy as vocation.

Conclusion

It is not within the scope of this presentation to

trace developments of church and state relations throughout the ensuing periods of Mennonite history from the seventeenth to the twentieth centuries. A general oversimplification would be to say that Dutch, German, and Swiss Mennonites in that order moved from the traditional Anabaptist position of church and state separation to acceptance of generally unquestioned participation in government, accompanied by the abandonment of nonresistance. German Mennonites in Russia were in a unique situation in having been given local autonomy, but in addition to this, in the early 1900's moved into a program of moderate political action, including the electing of members to the national parliament. Under Bolshevism, Mennonite communites were gradually disintegrated, the process being completed in World War II.

Again, to oversimplify further, American Mennonite views of church and state as represented by various Mennonite branches and by variations within the respective branches move along a spectrum of some range. The span is from a position of moderately extended political action, including voting, the holding of political office (usually involving non-coercive tasks, if it is possible to speak of such in light of the coercive principle of all government), in some cases participation in the military, to the absolutist position of complete withdrawal (if, of course, it is possible to speak of such in light of the "political" and "societal" nature of life, particularly in our contemporary scene).

Our discussion from here on will focus primarily on the peace witness of the *Mennonite Church* though by implication other Mennonite groups cannot be altogether excluded because of cooperative relations through which peace witness at times is given.

Peace Witness Documents of the Mennonite Church and Its Peace Agencies, 1915-66

The documents (see list in Bibliography) examined fall roughly into three classes:

1. Letters or direct presentations by church peace agencies or their officers to government officials on matters that have to do directly with the church's own relations to the state, particularly with regard to military training and participation in war.

2. Official statements of position largely formulated by church peace committees, approved and adopted by Mennonite General Conference, and designed for doctrinal self-clarification, peace education, and practical guidance for the brotherhood, as well as for instrumental use in peace witness to American Christianity, governmental authorities, and society at large, from the stance of biblical nonresistance.

3. Letters, telegrams, and similar messages to governmental authorities, pledging prayer and good will, encouraging peace and reconciliation among men and nations, and protesting injustices, bloodshed, or

other actions deemed to be under the judgment of God and detrimental to the welfare of persons.

In the following examination, no attempt is made to distinguish among the various types of documents. Rather they constitute parts of a whole. While personal letters to and from peace committee leaders and other supplementary material, such as study papers, have been read, the peace documents themselves are herein reviewed. First, features that remain constant throughout the 1915-66 period are noted. Second, perceptible changes and/or trends are observed. The next section of the paper then takes up the theological implications.

Features of Peace Witness Documents That Remain Constant

1. *Historic basis for witnessing.* Letters, presentations, and statements generally include (usually in their introduction) a pointed mention of the historic continuity of the Anabaptist-Mennonite peace witness, which is given as a form of testimony in itself. This serves as an orientation as to who is speaking and as a justification for the right to speak, since the long persistence of the Mennonite peace testimony presumably reflects a certain maturity and depth of conviction growing out of experience. The more recent documents do not shy away from employing this historic relatedness, although it is less elaborated and referred to throughout the document rather than

forming a major introduction.

In other words, Mennonite peace witness has maintained its historical consciousness and bears witness out of the brotherhood's sense of commitment and experience.

2. *Biblical-Christological authority for witness.* The authority of the Scriptures is affirmed as the foundation of peace witness and equated with the authority of Christ and the message of the gospel. A constant feature is that biblical authority is interpreted in the light of the Spirit and teachings of Christ and His suffering example as the highest revelation of God's will and in the light of the finality of the New Testament as the norm of doctrine and life for the Christian. Peace witness is understood to be an integral part of the ministry of the gospel although we will note later how this becomes more implicit in the more recent documents.

3. *Attitude of nonresistance.* The tenor of peace witness reflected by the documents is one of nonresistance and willingness to suffer (the "way of the cross"), rather than demanding rights or expressing harsh judgment. That is, the manner of witness seems to remain constantly compatible with the nature of the gospel it seeks to represent. The way of love is set forth as being "at the heart of the gospel."

4. *Contemporary orientation.* All letters, presentations, and statements are formulated within a particular historical setting and exhibit to a greater or

lesser degree an orientation to their contemporary scene. For example, the March 2, 1927, Peace Problems Committee letter to the Senate Foreign Relations Committee chairman speaks of difficulties in Mexico and Nicaragua and of the movement of gunboats to China. The 1937 "Statement on Peace, War, and Military Service," talks of war bonds and the possibility of conscription. The 1951 "Declaration" mentions atomic blasts along with "scientific, educational, and cultural programs designed to contribute to war." Since 1940, and particularly since 1950, documents deal more at length with specific areas of concern such as statements on "Industrial Relations" (1941), "Race Relations" (1955), "Communism and Anti-Communism" (1961), and "Witness to the State" (1961). Along with this, letters more recently deal with a wider range of concerns than national and international peace and military conscription.

5. *Attitude toward the state.* The basic right and function of the state to maintain an orderly society are recognized as being ordered of God. Respect for those in authority is expressed. Obedience to God through submission to proper state requirements is upheld as a Christian obligation, but is qualified with such phrases as: " . . . except in such cases where obedience to the government would cause us to violate the teachings of the Scriptures so that we could not maintain a clear conscience before God" ("Peace,

War, and Military Service," 1937). A strong emphasis is on the unqualified position that the Christian cannot participate in the execution of force, even though the state is granted the necessity of coercive power. Prayer for authorities is promised frequently to those addressed.

6. *View of man and the social order.* It is clear that man and the social order are regarded to be in the condition of sin and rebellion against God and in need of redemption through the gospel. Acceptance of the gospel, the power and rule of Christ, and regeneration of life are seen as necessary to the reconciliation of men. "These declarations of faith and conviction give no blueprint for permanent peace, nor do they assume that human endeavor alone can bring about a warless and sinless world within history" ("Declaration" of 1951). However, discipleship to Christ is seen as calling for "an action program requiring the full unfolding of divine grace and power through man . . . the only hope of the world" (*Ibid.*) "The gospel is not mere idealism" ("Race Relations," 1955).

7. *Recurring points of witness.* War is without qualification declared sin and protested, but governments engaging therein are not condemned outright. The way of peace is set forth as the will of God for individuals and society as well as for the Christian. Actions of governmental authorities which promote peace within the nation or among nations,

25

such as disarmament, are commended and encouraged. Actions which reflect war preparations, such as conscription or warlike activity, are protested. The non-resistant position of the Mennonite Church as a response to the claims of Christ is often stated. Requests are made to government to consider the Christian conscience and to provide for its exercise.

Throughout the entire period, 1915-66, periodic letters and messages (including one widely signed petition) to governmental officials by Mennonite General Conference, Peace Problems Committee, and Committee on Peace and Social Concerns, go beyond witnessing to the church's own position of nonresistance and approve or protest governmental policy. Examples are: The 1915 General Conference letter to President Wilson commending peace efforts with regard to Mexico and Nicaragua; the 1921 Peace Problems report of a petition against universal military conscription; the 1927 Peace Problems Committee letter to William E. Borah, Chairman of the Senate Foreign Relations Committee, expressing views on a number of national and international policy points; the 1929 General Conference letter to President Hoover and to the Prime Minister of Canada commending the signing of a Peace Pact; the 1930 cablegram sent by the Peace Problems Committee chairman to the American Delegation at the London Naval Conference; the 1933 cablegram to the Geneva Disarmament Conference; the Mennonite Central Committee letter to

President Roosevelt in 1937 by Mennonite Church representatives, citing favorably the President's peace declarations. More recent communications are the 1963 General Conference letter to President Kennedy supporting the nuclear weapons test ban treaty and proposed civil rights measures, and the 1965 General Conference telegram to President Johnson, "to register with you our deep concerns and misgivings regarding both the moral basis and the direction of American policy there."

A positive concern and willingness to aid in ministering to the needs of mankind in wartime and peacetime are frequently expressed in correspondence, presentations, and statements. During the years just prior to World War II, much attention is given to testimony concerning conscription and presentations of alternate service plans to United States and Canadian governmental officials in cooperation with other historic peace churches.

Trends Reflected in Peace Witness Documents

1. *More elaboration of bases for peace witness.* The documents under examination show a progressively increasing attempt to elaborate and interpret more definitively what is meant by the bases of peace witness with regard to the authority of the Scriptures, the way of the cross, the rule of Christ, Christian discipleship, and the nature of the church, the state, and church-state relations, and the nature

of Christian witness to the state. While there is an expected concentration on particular foci rather than doctrinal treatment, the earlier documents say nothing of the nature of the church, little about the state, suggest no eschatological perspective, speak not at all of the resurrection, and generally omit the aspect of witness that is concerned with winning men to faith in Christ.

2. *Peace witness expanded to include wider areas of concern.* Documents over the period gradually attempt to spell out more fully the implications of peace witness as related to more and broader areas. They seem to have in view a wider audience. Earlier documents are almost exclusively related to witnessing against war and war trends or preparations, particularly conscription and military training. More recent documents expand peace witness to include such areas of concern as economic and labor relations, social conditions, race relations, attitudes and notions regarding atheistic ideologies, capital punishment, rehabilitation of released prisoners. In addition to speaking toward the brotherhood and governmental authorities, they seem to be more consciously addressing other Christians and society at large.

This trend coincides with the successive formation of Mennonite Church peace agencies, namely: Military Problems Committee (1907-19); Peace Problems Committee (1919-65); Committee on Industrial Relations (1939-51), renamed the Committee on Social and Economic Relations (1951-65), and the merging of the Peace Problems Committee and Committee on Social and Economic Relations to form the present Committee on Peace and Social Concerns (1965-). Paralleling this development within the Mennonite Church is the formation and growth of the inter-Mennonite peace, material aid, and service agency, the Mennonite Central Committee (1920-).

The expanding interest in social issues parallels also the rise of national and international concern with questions of social and political justice and the increasing attention given the same by the Christian churches. Further, the more intense concentration of effort to extend the peace witness represents a continuation and more activated implementation of the original intent of the Peace Problems Committee to carry out a program of (a) peace education within the church; (b) keeping government informed of our peace position; and (c) peace witness to other Christians. See Peace Problems Committee report to General Conference, 1927. Point (b) was explained to mean: "To represent the church and her position on this doctrine before any departments of our state, provincial, and national governments which have to do with legislation or the enforcement of legislation affecting our status as nonresistant Christians and to encourage officials wherever possible in a wider application of the policy of goodwill rather than that of force and war."

3. *Increasingly forward-looking stance of peace witness.* While there is a continuation of relating peace witness to the historic experience of the Anabaptist-Mennonite brotherhood, the direction pointed to is increasingly forward. Positive statements of what we "mean to do" become more numerous and proportionately begin to equal and then surpass what we "cannot do." The tenor of this trend is expressed in the 1951 "Declaration":

"While we are deeply grateful to God for the precious heritage of faith, including the principle of love and nonresistance, which our Swiss, Dutch, and German Anabaptist-Mennonite forefathers purchased for us by their faith, obedience, and sacrifice, and which we believe is again expressed in the above declarations and commitments, we are convinced that this faith must be repossessed personally by each one out of his own reading and obeying of God's Word, and must ever be wrought out in practice anew. Hence we summon our brotherhood to a deeper mastery of the Scriptures as the infallible revelation of God's will for us, and to find afresh under Holy Spirit guidance its total message regarding Christ's way and its application in our present world."

4. *Appearance of confession and repentance.* In more recent documents, the note of confession and repentance appears, and the posture of identification with the ills of society is more directly taken, while at the same time a stronger note of the victorious character of the Christian hope is sounded.

5. *Peace witness beyond statements of Mennonite*

position of nonresistance is associated more explicitly with the gospel. As noted earlier, from the very beginning of the period, 1915-66, direct witness is given (largely by letter) to governmental authorities with regard to national and international legislation, actions, and policies on specific issues. In the earlier documents, the basis for such witness is seen to lie in Christian responsibility to bear testimony to the state concerning the sanctity of human life, the desirability of maintaining peace among men and liberty of conscience, and the assumption that governmental leaders in formulating national and international policies can take peace principles seriously. The theological rationale for witness to the state is not spelled out.

In more recent documents, the bases emphasized for direct witness to the state are that all men need to be called to salvation through faith in Christ and to discipleship to Him, that all men stand under the norm and judgment of one morality as set forth by Christ regardless of their recognition of it or response to it, that witness to the state is part of the gospel message of the lordship of Christ, and that it is Christian obligation to hold before authorities the moral implications of their actions under God.

In more recent documents there is a pronounced increase of emphasis on the evangelistic-reconciliation intent and the personal aspects of Christian peace witness to the state and the social order, as

31

for example, "that we accept our obligation and privilege to bring in love the saving gospel to communists everywhere, as well as to all men, and to win them for Christ" ("Communism and Anti-Communism," 1961). "The love of Christ constrains us to a ministry of reconciliation which extends to all men, including those in government . . . witness (1) concerning faith in Him, that whosoever will may come; (2) concerning the meaning of true discipleship . . . ; (3) concerning the love of God for all men . . ." ("Part II. The Christian Witness to the State," 1961). "We are convinced that the teachings of Jesus and the power of the gospel are the solution to the problems of sin in man and society; and that the reason society is still in its broken state is either because men reject Christ and His gospel or because those who have taken the name of Christ will not live that gospel . . ." ("Declaration," 1951).

6. *In summary, the following may be most pertinent.* (a) Although the issues toward which peace witness is oriented have to some extent been continually changing with changing historical situations, there does not seem to be a divergence from the historic-Anabaptist-Mennonite nature of peace witness positions *insofar as those positions were developed and clarified theologically.* That is, on the level of actual performance, Mennonite peace witness, 1915-66, has not changed in nature, but in degree of intensification and expansion into wider areas of concern. (b)

The trends noted in peace witness documents reflect an underlying attempt to come more seriously to grips with the theological bases of Anabaptist-Mennonite peace witness which either have not been adequately developed or not fully resolved in the past. (c) The expansion of peace witness into broader areas and the spelling out of theological under-standings more explicitly have brought into focus basic questions which were implicit in earlier peace witness but are now being articulated in the context of contemporary church-state issues.

Some Observations on Theological Implications of Trends in Recent Peace Witness Documents

This section is not an attempt to make a comprehensive theological analysis, but rather to lift out several pivotal points which give peace witness documents since about 1950 their theological complexion.

The 1961 statement, "Part II. The Christian Witness to the State," is perhaps the most careful presentation of the current Mennonite peace witness stance and reflects its underlying theological assumptions. That document is the main (though not the only) reference point of our present discussion since it is representative of our studies, consultations, and documents of peace witness that reflect the present theological direction of Mennonite peace witness.

1. *The theology of church and world, and church and state, in contemporary Mennonite peace witness is developed from the perspective of church-world and church-state separation, but is directed toward church-world and church-state relationships.* This

is related to our previous conclusion, namely, that the most discernible trend in recent peace documents is the attempt to deal with questions and underlying theological assumptions not clarified or fully resolved in the past. Traditional Anabaptist-Mennonite dealing with church-world and church-state issues has been primarily from the standpoint of the conflicts involved and the question of how separation is to be maintained. Now, the question occupying chief attention is how and on what theological premise the church is to fulfill her ministry of reconciliation and witness in relation to the world and state.

This is not to say that there is less contemporary concern with questions of church-world and church-state separation, but the concentration is on providing a theological basis for "positive" (that is not to imply "compatible" or "cooperative") connections. Early Anabaptists and later Mennonites dealt with church-state "connections" largely through the question of participation versus nonparticipation in government by officeholding, and also in the case of American Mennonites, the question of voting versus nonvoting. These questions are rather curiously almost absent from current Mennonite peace witness documents, or perhaps more accurately, they have been absorbed into the question as to how Christians are to function within the structures of society at large.

The present attention is on the witness of the church within the framework of church-world (including the state) relationships. The theological intent underlying recent peace documents looks beyond the maintenance of church-state separation per se and attempts to answer questions not raised as seriously heretofore in order to provide a consistently biblical rationale for Mennonite peace witness.

2. *The nature and function of the church are seen as essentially distinct from, but thereby relevant to, the world and state.* Recent peace documents share with the past in emphasizing that the church's primary calling is to be the church. It is assumed by current peace witness theology that the church is a "free church." There is no hint that church and state can be or should be one unified order. Any cooperation or relation cannot be one of "kind." The radical distinction of church and state in both nature and function is affirmed. The state partakes of the fallen nature of the "world," but is nevertheless the servant or instrument of God in His ordering of society. The church is the community of converted believers which lives under obedience to Christ as His body and is the particular locus of His redemptive work in the world.

But for the church to be the church, is not viewed from the standpoint of withdrawal and isolation. Rather the church being herself means that she is a redeemed community taking part in God's reconciling action in the world and represents a new reality in history. Her ministry of reconciliation and witness grow out of the nature of her redeemed being and take form as she lives in relation to the world. The nature of the church, then, is defined not in terms of pietistic experience only but in terms of a new order of life which has come into history through Christ (the kingdom of Christ), and which continues to become visible through the church in the world.

In relation to the state, the church is not one power institution confronting another. It is rather the witness of a redeemed brotherhood of new life under voluntary obedience to Christ, to a power structure that partakes of the fallen nature of the "world" with its rebellion against God. The very fact of their clearly differing natures creates a distinct separation of church and state which at the same time makes possible their confrontation without confusion of roles. The more clearly the duality of church and state is seen with regard to their respective natures and functions, the more free the church becomes to confront the state (one might even say, "cooperative with" at times in an understood sense), and the more uniquely relevant her ministry and witness are. The state is not then being threatened nor its tasks assumed by a rival power institution but is faced with a "witness" to another reality (the kingdom of Christ made visible in the church) which gives a perspective to the state's own functions that it could not receive in any other way.

The state may still react negatively to this confrontation because it misunderstands the nature of the church's witness to be a power challenge, or because it rejects the divine reality the church represents. The church nevertheless understands this reaction and accepts its suffering consequences as a means of clarifying further both her own nature and function and also that of the state. It is in this encounter of the church with the "world," and the church with the state, that the nature of each is revealed, a truth originally made clear by the event of the cross. In this encounter the "world" and state are brought to recognize a divine reality beyond their own horizon of understanding.

The point of this discussion is mainly: That the theology underlying recent witness documents is not *derived from* the concept of "contemporary relevance." It is rather the position that *because of* the nature and function of the church as over against the nature and function of the state, the church *is* (not must be "made") relevant to the state, and that this relevance constitutes part of the basis for witness to the state.

3. *The function of and witness to the state is seen within the framework of the redemptive purpose of God.* One aspect of the traditional Mennonite way

of speaking about church and state is the emphasis on their two different purposes or realms of operation. The church is the minister of the gospel to win men to faith in Christ, and the state is the minister of law to preserve order among sinful men. A point not emphasized until recent peace documents, however, is that church and state are not only parallel lines of divine operation in the world, but that both stand together, though in radically different ways, within the redemptive purpose and plan of God. An example of biblical support for this is found in 1 Timothy 2:1-4. Christians are to pray for state authorities. The authorities are to preserve a desirable order wherein Christians can function freely. This is God's will and has in view His seeking "all men to be saved and to come to the knowledge of the truth."

It follows that Christian witness to the state is not then simply an enlightened church telling the state how to function in its separate realm for the natural good of all. Rather, the church's witness has in view that the state's role in the divine ordering of God lies in His redemptive plan made known in Christ.

This may be said to be implicit in early Anabaptist-Mennonite insistence that for governmental authorities to fulfill properly their function requires that they provide for religious liberty. If religious liberty for Christians is for the ultimate purpose of ministering the gospel (which is clear in the minds of early Anabaptists), then to petition the state for the free exercise of faith is in effect telling governmental authorities that they are responsible to cooperate with the redemptive plan of God, although it is not their task to implement it since by nature the state is not qualified for that. Anabaptist witnessing made this point, while at the same time maintaining clearly that although both church and state stand within the divine purpose of God in history, only the church can embody the accomplishment of that purpose, while the state's character and ministry are always "outside the perfection of Christ." The redemptive perspective is not clear in earlier peace documents of the 1915-66 period. Therefore, neither is the theological basis of peace witness to the state. Rulers are viewed to be ministers of God in the sense that they help bring evildoers to the consequence of their own evil as required by God's law of cause and effect which operates in society. The state is therefore seen only as part of a divinely created natural order of things not within the framework of redemption.

The important point in this discussion is that witness to the state is currently seen as growing out of the claims of the gospel upon all men and is not based on the concept that the state operates under a separate natural law of divine Providence which lies outside of the church's concern or mandate. From this position is derived the concept that the church must give witness at those points where the state, as it functions, is incompatible with the reconciliation of the world to God in Christ, and positively where the state, whether it acknowledges it or not, is serving the fact of reconciliation of the world by God in Christ.

Closely related is the "middle axioms" concept of witness. This means that the state cannot be expected to understand the redemptive purpose which is the ultimate purpose for its use by God in the ordering of society, nor can the state function by the love ethic of the gospel and the church because the state partakes of the nature of fallen society. The church, nevertheless, witnesses to the state from the viewpoint of redemptive understanding and the *agape* love ethic. The points on which the church then addresses the state may in themselves *seem* to be only "natural" or humanitarian norms of civil justice, but from the perspective of the church they are norms which have their ultimate reference point in the redemptive plan of God. These norms derived from redemptive understanding and the love ethic, but which are spoken to only on the level of the state's understanding and achievement possibilities in specific situations, are the "middle axiom" points of peace witness to the state.

It may be suggested here that the present trend toward greater intensification of the church's peace witness to the state as well as with regard to other structures of society may be justified to the extent that it remains consistent with its own perspective of redemptive purpose and that it retains the character of the Christian love ethic. We may recall also our previous observation that the more recent peace documents reflect a conscious attempt to clarify our peace witness more fully in terms of calling men to personal faith and discipleship, along with "a witness which reasons with them 'of righteousness, of temperance, and of judgment.'" The effort to place peace witness to the state on a more fully developed theological base has, therefore, served to clarify the direct relation of this kind of witness to the task of evangelism even in its more narrow sense.

However, the question may be seriously raised as to whether the church continues to witness out of her own nature and experience when she undertakes to translate absolute norms of redemptive love into relative performance norms for the state. Or does the church in her witness then take on the character of judgment rather than reconciliation, and by extending her witness beyond her experience invalidate its own authenticity?

The theology underlying contemporary Mennonite peace witness documents would answer this question by placing it within the context of the meaning of the lordship of Christ.

4. *The lordship of Christ over the "powers" of*

43

the world is basic to the premise that peace witness to the state is an integral part of the gospel. The interpretation of the lordship of Christ represented in recent peace documents is that Christ is Lord over both the church which recognizes His lordship and the world (including the state) which denies it. This position in relation to the state is based on an exegetical interpretation of Romans 13:1-7 that sees spiritual powers (the *exousiai*) standing behind human authorities in government so that there is an integral relationship between spiritual powers and earthly rulers. To this is joined the *Heilsgeschichte* interpretation of the New Testament which sees the death and resurrection of Christ as the midpoint of history when the spiritual and earthly powers combined to crucify the Lord but were overthrown in His resurrection, though not as yet destroyed. This event means that the powers now standing behind the "world" order, and in particular behind governmental authorities, are subject to Christ in the sense that their ultimate power is broken. But since these powers will not be destroyed (by Christ) until the final consummation, they are still in rebellion against God. The present period of Christ's reign is one of tension between the victory already won and its culmination yet to come. But the new reality that now overarches the whole of history is the reign of Christ which is moving toward its consummation.

The "already" and "not yet" existing at the same

time explains how the state can at one and the same be good and bad; good, in that the powers have been subjected by Christ's death and resurrection to serve His purpose (represented by the state in its functioning as described in Romans 13). This situation may give the state at times the appearance of having broken out of its subjection (the state as in Revelation 13).

This view of the lordship of Christ is the theological justification for the position that the state is ordained ("ordered") to serve the redemptive plan of God. Rather than being an absolute entity which functions under God, it is a universal order of creation, essentially unrelated to Christ's redemptive work in history. The state is to be obeyed, then, not because it is a sacred institution as such, but because it is instrumental in God's ordering of the world toward His redemptive purpose in Christ who is Lord of all. The state in recent peace documents is not spoken of as "ordained of God," which in the past has carried the connotation of a divine institutional entity representing a natural moral order of creation. The concept is rather that the state as a structure of society (taking varied specific forms) is "ordered" by God. This ordering is not by some general "natural law" built into the created universe, but an ordering through the lordship of Christ. He having broken the powers of "this age" is now in the process of subduing all things to Himself and bringing to fulfillment the new age of His kingdom.

At this point we may recall Hans Hillerbrand's observation that the particular understanding of the Scriptures that underlies the Anabaptist view of the Christian and state relations is that the coming of Christ has brought about a new situation (page 3). But concepts of Mennonite peace witness diverge primarily at the theological point as to whether the locus of Christ's lordship is only in the church where His rule has been accepted, thereby delivering believers from bondage to the powers of "this world," or whether His lordship applies also to the whole cosmic order under the rubric of redemption.

The former view holds that Christ's lordship means His conquest *in men* by which they are saved from bondage to the powers. The latter contends that this individual deliverance is not possible unless something has happened to the powers themselves to break their absolute hold on men. In the former view, the witness of the gospel is that in Christ men who believe are delivered from the bondage of the powers of the world, but the powers remain unchanged in status. In the latter view, the witness of the gospel is that the powers that bind men have been defeated and although they can and do still enslave men, men are potentially free and must be pointed to their freedom in Christ. It would seem that these two views should not be irreconcilable since one emphasizes the subjective aspect of Christ's lordship, and the other the objective aspect as prior.

The point with regard to peace witness is that if the lordship of Christ applies only to believers, then peace witness to the state can be speaking to governmental authorities only of their personal salvation by receiving the forgiveness of Christ and regeneration of life. But if Christ is Lord over both church and world, witness to governmental authorities becomes a part of the gospel message proclaiming a new age for men to enter through faith in the victory of Christ which is now in the process of being fulfilled. Men are called personally to faith in Christ, but they are called also to recognize that their actions now stand under the rule of Christ and will be judged according to the purposes and norms of His kingdom when He is building in the world.

The lordship of Christ over both church and world has the merit of giving a Christological perspective to the meaning of history and the working of God in the world. It plants the peace witness squarely in the historical fact of the reconciliation of the world to God in Christ. However, although the *Heilsge-schichte* eschatology gives more place to the significance of the final *eschaton* than "realized eschatology" does, the question may still be raised as to whether this perspective of our present age is too optimistic and thereby misleading with regard to the potential action of the church in the world.

There is also the problem that the lordship of

Christ over the world means He is also working in the world redemptively apart from His body. The church cannot discern and witness to His working outside of herself without herself entering into the situation where this action may be taking place. To do this requires that the church identify herself with the "world" in a given situation in order to witness to the working of Christ there. This is where Mennonite peace witness runs into difficulty. For if the church is to witness to the action of Christ taking place in the world apart from herself, it must become actually identified with the sinful order where that action is occurring. Then it can experience and bear witness to the reconciliation and justification of God in Christ at that point in history. This concept partakes of Bonhoeffer's ethics of justification through identification with Christ as true man in the world, and does not take as seriously as Mennonites do, the absolute norms involved in obedience to Christ.

However, Mennonite peace witness theology seeks to clarify this problem in its concept of ethics.

5. *The theology underlying recent peace witness documents holds that there is one morality under which church and world (including the state) stand, and that the difference is in the response to the one divine will, not in a difference of standards for the church and world (or state).* The *agape* love ethic revealed in Christ by the cross is the standard

of God's will for all men. It is expected that Christians will respond obediently to this ethic, or more correctly, to Christ as the absolute revelation of God's will.

On the other hand, it is expected that the "world" of fallen society will reject the norm of *agape* love as a criterion for ethical action and that the state to a greater or lesser degree partakes in that rejection. Christians then have a twofold calling. First, they are to be the ministers of reconciliation by their life of love in obedience to Christ, which involves the faithful practice of giving oneself for his brother and in service to one's neighbor. This is the priestly mission of the church. Second, Christians are to be witnesses, calling all of society, including the state, to account for its conduct in keeping with the will of God as made known through Christ. This is the prophetic mission of the church. Mennonite peace witness documents of recent date especially, distinguish between these two functions of the church's action in the world.

Christian ethics is to be practiced by Christians as integral to the gospel which they bear. The nature of the church's ministry in the world must always be identified with a life that partakes of the nature of God's reconciliation of men as revealed in the cross, and that gives evidence of the power of the resurrection. Although the nonresistant Christian recognizes that his expression of self-giving love and his new life of resurrection power are never perfect in performance, he believes they are perfected in Christ and refuses to change his ethical frame of reference to the relative morality of the social order. The ethical concept underlying Mennonite peace witness emphasizes both identification with the brokenness of men standing in need of the forgiveness of Christ and at the same time identification with Christ in the new triumphant life of the resurrection which is not oriented to the sinful state of man. The victory of Christ is a present reality.

In the performance of its priestly and prophetic functions, Mennonite peace witness seeks to follow the normative example of Christ's ministry by calling rebellious society to the judgment of God's will while at the same time serving it from within through *agape* love. This would seem to be a fair characterization of the Anabaptist-Mennonite paradoxical ethic of "separation" and love.

At this point a final brief comment on the implications of the modern welfare state and the secularization of society may be in order.

6. *Peace witness documents reflect an awareness of the modern welfare state and the secularization of society, but subordinate these factors to biblical and theological understandings of the nature and function of church and state.* Against the background of our foregoing discussions on the nature of the church and state, we may understand how secular-

50

ization of the state and society can be seen in a positive way. The nature of the church is of a divine order, but the nature of the state is "worldly" though divinely ordered. Secularization reveals this true character of the state and thereby helps to clarify the nature of the church's relation to it.

Secularization is not *secularism*. The former is the process which desacralizes the concept of the state and "world" and reveals their true character. But *secularism* attempts to make *secularization* the ultimate norm for society and thereby again attributes to the state and "world" an absolute autonomy rather than subordination to God. The church therefore sees the possibility of positive relations with the secular state which cooperates with its divine ordering, but opposes the state that is sacralized by religious self-pretensions including secularism. It is the *corpus Christianum* concept of church and state that confuses their respective roles, for the state then is understood to have the nature of a divine order rather than a "worldly" order divinely ordered. Cooperation then takes on the form of an unequal yoke as though it were an equal yoke.

The modern welfare functions of the state are recognized by recent peace documents as well as the secularization trends. However, these are not yet seen as factors that essentially alter the basic concepts of church and state relations. The sword-character of the state is still assumed to be primarily in focus and

secularization is always viewed cautiously because of
its always being on the potential verge of secularism.

Summary and Conclusion

The previous section has attempted to locate some pivotal points of peace witness documents that have theological implications. Do these contemporary theological assumptions represent a change from Anabaptist-Mennonite historical positions? Some comment on this question has been given along the way.

From 1915 to about 1940, the peace documents appear to assume the doctrinal understandings developed and consolidated by Mennonite Church leaders during the previous period, 1875-1914. *Bible Doctrine*, edited by Daniel Kauffman, was first published in 1914 as the first attempt by American Mennonites to compile a more or less comprehensive treatment of biblical teachings. From 1940 to 1950, some new questions were faced through the experience of World War II, Civilian Public Service, and the political, social, and technological developments of the period. These years are the beginning of an uneasy feeling that Mennonite peace witness was not rooted deeply enough theologically. Some attempt to begin working at this problem is reflected in the 1951 Statement of Mennonite General Conference.

From 1950 to the present, particularly from 1955 on, there seems to be a conscious attempt to come to grips with the theological question unresolved previously in Mennonite peace witness. If Mennonites themselves cannot function as governmental authorities, at least not in that which requires the use of the "sword," then on what basis can they presume to witness to those in office? Further, if they do speak, on what basis can Mennonites say anything to the state outside of contexts where their own nonresistant principles apply? The present theological positions were formed largely in relation to these questions. Though we have spoken primarily to witness to the state, the same questions and theological problems are implicit in the relations of Christians with and their witness to other social structures of society. The first aspect of change in the theology of peace witness documents, therefore, is that the more recent documents are oriented to questions which were only implicit in peace witness up to 1950 but became gradually more explicit thereafter and were directly faced from 1955 on.

Closely related to the point above is the conclusion that up to at least 1950 peace witness documents addressed to the state on disarmament and other policies do not exhibit a very clear theological rationale and are not supported by other peace documents giving this rationale since none is available. In other words, peace witness that goes beyond explanation of the church's own nonresistant position does not appear to altogether fit the concepts of church and state that were assumed by the Mennonite Church in that period. This may be due to various reasons. The Peace Problems Committee may not have been speaking out of brotherhood consensus. However, some of the messages to heads of state came from Mennonite General Conference, and all were reported to General Conference. The 1921 petition against military conscription had 20,000 signatures. The Drafting Committee of the General Conference letter to President Wilson in 1915 was composed of S. F. Coffman, J. E. Hartzler, and George R. Brunk, and the Peace Problems Committee behind the circulation of the 1921 Petition was composed of Aaron Loucks, S. G. Shetler, D. D. Miller, L. O. King, and E. L. Frey.

Dissent pertaining to this kind of witness to government does not seem to have been large-scale. What dissent there was came more from fears that Mennonite peace witness might ally itself too closely with groups representing liberal theology. There does not seem to be much questioning of Mennonite peace witness on the basis of church-state theology as such except by some individuals who differed on eschatological points.

Or it may be that the relation between peace witness to the state and church-state theology may not have been thought through coordinately, and so any discrepancies were not apparent. Very little space is given in the 1914 *Bible Doctrine*, for example, to a doctrine of the state, or to church-state relations, and what is there is written with little biblical exegesis or theological development. As late as 1948, Erland Waltner wrote in his doctoral dissertation introduction:

"Whereas considerable attention has been given to historical studies, almost nothing has been written on the biblical basis of the Mennonite attitude toward the state. Except for a few writings of Guy F. Hershberger, Edward Yoder, and Don E. Smucker, this area of study has been scarcely touched. Among Mennonite writers, moreover, differences in viewpoint on various aspects of church and state problems are evident."[13]

The misfit of Mennonite peace witness with its own church-state theology, 1915-50, may be explained in another way. The doctrinal positions developed in the earlier period, 1875-1914, partook to some extent of a fundamentalist cast of thought developed in reaction to nineteenth century liberalism. While Mennonite leaders were selective and critical, it is possible that their concern for the nonresistant position and peace witness was not worked out from sufficiently original theological standpoints. Thus while their biblical support for nonresistance was clear, their theological concept of witness to the state was not. As a result, when that witness was given beyond a defense of the church's nonresistant position, it had the appearance of moving into alien territory without sufficient awareness of the implications.

Still another view may be that the historical Anabaptist dynamic witness to the state was still showing itself alive in the Mennonite peace witness of 1915-50, but, separated by centuries from its original context, was not able to proceed with its earlier perspective and vitality and seemed out of place with the twentieth-century setting of Mennonites as the "quiet of the land."

In any case, by 1950 it was becoming clear that either an adequate theological undergirding for peace witness to the state must be developed, or else witness must be viewed primarily within the context of a "strategy of withdrawal." The change represented in peace documents from 1950, and especially from 1955 on, is not a change in actual performance of witness to the state, but reflects the decision to give such witness its necessary theological undergirding.

The question then becomes one of whether the theological positions developed, especially from 1955 on, remain faithful to basic biblical and Anabaptist-Mennonite understandings since the more recent concepts are moving on more unfamiliar ground.

Mennonite theology in the past has been built on selective borrowing and unique reconstruction. This is still going on. It is clear that the key theological ideas of the recent peace documents are formed with heavy leaning on Oscar Cullmann's exegetical and theological work. The *Heilsgeschichte* interpretation of the New Testament, the lordship of Christ over the powers as related to Romans 13, and the eschatological perspective given to state and church-state concepts are taken over from Cullmann almost intact. The influence of other views bearing on peace witness are discernible such as, for example, Karl Barth's concept that the church is relevant to the state by being the church as in the course of her life she creates institutions, patterns, and value judgments that the state may imitate to a degree. It must be fairly conceded that many of the theological points made by contemporary theology have considerable biblical validity. Nevertheless, the dangers are real and major. Mennonite peace witness theologians have not been unmindful of this.

Peace witness concepts derived from other sources have been checked for biblical verification. They have been placed into an Anabaptist-Mennonite framework that does not concede to relative situational ethics but continues to insist on the norm of biblical absolutes as interpreted from a Christological perspective. The authority of the Scriptures is reaffirmed. It is also clear that while the contemporary emphasis is on the relation of the redemptive work of Christ and the ministry of the church to the structures of society, the necessity of personal regeneration of life is specifically maintained. The prevailing view that for the church to be relevant in society today she must find her frame of reference for action within the sinful social order is not followed by Mennonite peace witness theology which continues to place involvement with the "world" on the basis of the reality of the new life in Christ and its actual ethical possibilities. In fact, one of the strengths of recent peace documents is the emphasis that the resurrected life is integrally related (as it is everywhere in the New Testament) to the way of the cross and is the perspective from which the way of the cross is to be viewed. Thus the heart-beat of Mennonite peace witness is still the Anabaptist theme that justification by grace and discipleship cannot be separated, and that both constitute one witness to Christ and His salvation.

The triumphant confession of the lordship of Christ over all, the eschatological tension of the redeemed church in the present age, and the calling of men, including governmental authorities, to faith and discipleship, and reasoning with them of justice and righteousness are not unfamiliar to sixteenth-century Anabaptism and, more important, are characteristic notes of the New Testament.

Since theology today is in a state of flux, our concern should be to seek earnestly for a consensus of understanding in the brotherhood through a sharing of the Spirit's gifts in serious discussion, attempting to avoid a polarizing of positions into stereotype judgments. The chief dangers we presently face may be these: (1) That we may attempt to establish the basis and direction of our peace witness purely by abstracting doctrine out of the Scripture without the proper awareness that this is in itself a historical process informed by historical presuppositions and developments and without the recognition that God is working in history and unfolding His will to the church in history as she follows Christ in obedient faith. Or the opposite danger: (2) That we may attempt to formulate our peace witness by taking as our primary frame of reference the contemporary historical situation rather than the greater historical reality of the new life in Christ as revealed through the Scriptures and thereby subordinate the ultimate norms of God's redemptive purpose and action to immediate responses of faith that are not sufficiently informed by propositional truth.

These two dangers suggest that finding the will of God requires a positive holding together both the need for revealed biblical norms of truth and the need for responding in obedient faith to God's working in our own day of history. It is the genius of Anabaptist-Mennonite theology that it takes seriously both the authority of biblical truth as such and its dynamic relation to the self-revelation of God in history.

Herein may be the way toward reaching a unity of faith in which Mennonite peace witness can discern the will of God and be a worthy successor to Anabaptist forebears whose Christ of the Bible was the living Christ of history calling them to discipleship and prophetic witness in the midst of their historical situation.

Footnotes

1. Harold S. Bender, *The Anabaptist Vision*, (Goshen, Indiana: Mennonite Historical Society, 1949), reprinted from *The Mennonite Quarterly Review*, April 1944.

2. *The Complete Writings of Menno Simons* (Scottdale: Herald Press, 1956), pp. 158, 186, 310.

3. Hans J. Hillerbrand, *Die politische Ethik des Oberdeutschen Taufertums*, University of Erlangen, 1957. Summary: "The Anabaptist View of the State," *The Mennonite Quarterly Review*, Vol. XXXII (1958), pp. 83-110.

4. This position is clearly supported, for example, by the Schleitheim Confession of 1527 in the Sixth Article: "We are agreed as follows concerning the sword: The sword is ordained of God outside the perfection of Christ. It punishes and puts to death the wicked, and guards and protects the good. In the Law the sword was ordained for the punishment of the wicked and for their death, and the same sword is now ordained to be used by the worldly magistrates." (Translated by J. C. Wenger, *Glimpses of Mennonite History and Doctrine*) (Scottdale: Herald Press, 1947, p. 210).

5. In the death sentence pronounced over Felix Manz on January 5, 1527, it was charged that he held that no Christian can carry out death sentence on any person nor put anyone to death. (John Horsch, *The Principle of Nonresistance as Held by the Mennonite Church*) (Scottdale: Mennonite Publishing House, 1927; Second Edition, 1940, p. 19).

Menno Simons argues against capital punishment on the ground that it denies to the transgressor the opportunity of repentance. He writes further: "Profane history shows that the Lacedaemonians, who were heathen, did not practice capital punishment, but they imprisoned their offenders and put them to work" (*The Complete Writings of Menno Simons*, "Epistle to Micron," pp. 920-22).

6. Hillerbrand, *op. cit.*, pp. 92, 93.

7. Hillerbrand's conclusion must here again be somewhat modified by the

less than absolute statements of Hans de Ries and Menno Simons, who consider the administering of civil office in a Christian manner extremely difficult but not necessarily impossible as the Swiss Brethren deemed it. This point is made by Erland Waltner in his unpublished doctoral dissertation, *An Analysis of the Mennonite View on the Christian's Relation to the State in the Light of the New Testament*, Eastern Baptist Theological Seminary, 1948, p. 99.

Hillerbrand (*op. cit.*, p. 101) himself also points to a minority within the Anabaptist movement who deviated from the mainstream rejection of office-holding.

8. Hillerbrand, *op. cit.*, pp. 95, 96.

9 Conrad Grebel's letter to Thomas Muntzer, September 5, 1524, translated by Harold S. Bender, *Conrad Grebel* (Mennonite Historical Society, 1950), p. 285.

10. Quoted by Harold S. Bender, *The Anabaptist Vision*, p. 21.

11. See Franklin H. Littell, "The Anabaptist Doctrine of the Restitution of the True Church," *Mennonite Quarterly Review*, Vol. XXIV (1950), p. 49.

12. Claus Felbinger's Confession Addressed to the Council of Waldshut (1560), *Mennonite Quarterly Review*, Vol. XXIX (1955), p. 145.

13. Erland Waltner, *An Analysis of the Mennonite Views on the Christian's Relation to the State*, p. 22.

Bibliography

Mennonite Peace Witness Documents, 1915-66

1915 Letter to President Wilson by Mennonite General Conference.

1921 Peace Problems Committee Petition to Congress (20,000 signatures).

1927 Peace Problems Committee Chairman's Letter to William E. Borah, Chairman of the Senate Foreign Relations Committee.

1930 Peace Problems Committee Cablegram to the American Delegation at the London Naval Conference.

1930 Peace Problems Committee Chairman's Letter to Simeon D. Fess, United States Senator from Ohio.

1933 Mennonite Peace Committee (Peace Problems Committee) Cablegram to Geneva Disarmament Conference.

1936 Mennonite Peace Manifesto (signed by International Mennonite leaders).

1937 *Peace, War, and Military Service:* A Statement of Position Adopted by Mennonite General Conference, at Turner, Oregon.

1937 Mennonite Central Committee Letter to President Roosevelt (including a Statement of Principles).

1939 Plan of Action for Mennonites in Case of War, prepared by the Mennonite Central Peace Committee.

1940 Letter to President Roosevelt (conjointly signed by Society of Friends, Mennonite Church, and Church of the Brethren Representatives).

1940 A Memorandum to the Government Regarding a Plan of Procedure for Providing Alternative Service for Conscientious Objectors in Case of Military Conscription.

1943 Statement of Policy, Mennonite Civilian Public Service, approved by Mennonite Central Committee.

1951 A *Declaration of Christian Faith and Commitment with Respect to Peace, War, and Nonresistance*: A Statement Adopted by Mennonite General Conference, at Goshen, Indiana.

1955 *The Way of Christian Love in Race Relations:* A Statement Adopted by Mennonite General Conference, at Hesston, Kansas.

1961 *The Christian Witness to the State:* A Statement of Position Adopted by Mennonite General Conference, at Johnstown, Pennsylvania.

1961 *Communism and Anti-Communism:* A Statement of Position Adopted by Mennonite General Conference, at Johnstown, Pennsylvania.

1963 Telegram to John F. Kennedy by Mennonite General Conference, at Kalona, Iowa.

1965 *Capital Punishment and the Ministry of the Church to the Offender:* A Statement Adopted by Mennonite General Conference, at Kidron, Ohio.

1965 A *New Look at the Church and State Issue:* Statements of Findings from the Church-State Study Conference, sponsored by Mennonite Central Committee, at Chicago, October 7-9, 1965.

1966 Notes from Consultation on "Faithfulness to Christ in Situations of International Conflict," sponsored by Mennonite Central Committee Peace Section, at Minneapolis, Minnesota, December 2-4, 1966.

1966 A Summary Review of the Witness of the Mennonite Church, Through the Committee on Peace and Social Concerns and Its Predecessors, to Other Christians, to the State, and to Society, with Respect to Peace, and the Social Implications of the Gospel (1915-66). Prepared by Guy F. Hershberger, December 1, 1966.

1967 A Summary Review of Questions Raised Concerning the Work of the CPSC and Its Predecessors, Particularly Concerning Witness to Other Christians, to the State, and to Society, with Respect to Peace and the Social Implications of the Gospel, and Concerning Inter-

Denominational Cooperation in Carrying on This Work (1925-66). Prepared by Guy F. Hershberger, January 20, 1967.

1967 International Conflict and the Church. A Statement of Findings from Consultation on "Faithfulness to Christ in Situations of International Conflict," sponsored by Mennonite Central Committee Peace Section, at Minneapolis, Minnesota, December 2-4, 1966; published in *Gospel Herald* (Scottdale, Pa.), Jan. 17, 1967.

Books

Barth, Karl, *Church and State*. London: Student Christian Movement Press, 1939.

——————, *Community, Church, and State*. New York: Doubleday & Co., 1960.

Brunner, Emil, *The Divine Imperative*. Philadelphia: The Westminster Press, 1947.

Bennett, John C., *Christians and the State*. New York: Charles Scribner's Sons, 1958.

Bainton, Roland, *Christian Attitudes Toward War and Peace*. New York: Abingdon Press, 1960.

Bonhoeffer, Dietrich, *Ethics*. Edited by Eberhard Bethge, New York: The Macmillan Co., 1962.

Braaten, Carl E., *New Directions in Theology Today*, Vol. II, "History and Hermeneutics." Philadelphia: The Westminster Press, 1966.

Cadoux, C. J., *The Early Christian Attitude Toward War*. London: Headley Bros., 1919.

Cullmann, Oscar, *The State in the New Testament*. New York; Charles Scribner's Sons, 1956.

——————, *Christ and Time*. London: SCM Press, Ltd., 1951.

Henry, Carl F. H., *The Protestant Dilemma*. Grand Rapids: Wm. Eerdmans, 1949.

——————, *The Uneasy Conscience of Modern Fundamentalism*. Grand Rapids: Wm. Eerdmans, 1947.

Gingerich, Melvin, *Service for Peace*. Akron, Pa.: Mennonite Central Committee, 1949.

Hershberger, Guy F., *War, Peace, and Nonresistance*. Scottdale: Herald Press, 1953.

——————, *The Way of the Cross in Human Relations*. Scottdale: Herald Press, 1958.

——————, Editor, *The Recovery of the Anabaptist Vision*. Scottdale: Herald Press, 1957.

Horsch, John, *Mennonites in Europe*. Scottdale: Mennonite Publishing House, 1950.

Kauffman, Daniel, Editor, *Bible Doctrine*. Scottdale: Mennonite Publishing House, 1914. Revised, *Doctrines of the Bible*, 1928.

Lasserre, Jean, *War and the Gospel*. Scottdale: Herald Press, 1962.

Lehmann, Paul, *Ethics in a Christian Context*, New York: Harper & Row, 1963.

Littell, Franklin, *From State Church to Pluralism*. New York: Doubleday and Co., 1962.

Maritain, Jacques, *Man and the State*. Chicago: University of Chicago Press, 1951. 1963 Edition (Phoenix Books).

Niebuhr, Reinhold, *Moral Man and Immoral Society*. New York: Charles Scribner's Sons, 1941.

Morrison, Clinton, *The Powers That Be*. London: SCM Press, Ltd., 1960.

Penner, Archie, *The Christian, the State, and the New Testament*. Altona, Manitoba: D. W. Friesen & Sons, Ltd., 1959.

Rutenber, Culbert G., *The Dagger and the Cross*. New York: Fellowship Publications, 1950.

Sanders, Thomas G., *Protestant Concepts of Church and State*. New York: Holt, Rinehart, and Winston, 1964.

Toews, Abram P., *The Problem of Mennonite Ethics*. Grand Rapids: Wm. B. Eerdmans Publishing Co., 1963.

Wenger, John C., *Glimpses of Mennonite History and Doctrine*. Scottdale: Herald Press, 1947.

——————, *Introduction to Theology*. Scottdale: Herald Press, 1954.

Pamphlets

Bender, Harold S. *The Anabaptist Vision*. Goshen: Mennonite Historical Society, 1949.

Horsch, John, *The Principle of Nonresistance as Held by the Mennonite Church*. Scottdale: Mennonite Publishing House, 1940.

Kik, J. Marcellus. *Church and State in the New Testament* Grand Rapids: Baker Book House, 1962.

Morrison, Clinton, *The Mission of the Church and Civil Govern-ment.* The Church Peace Mission, Washington, D.C.

Peachey, Paul, *Peace Is the Will of God,* A Statement Pre-pared by the Historic Peace Churches and the Inter-national Fellowship of Reconciliation, October, 1953.

Yoder, John H., *Reinhold Niebuhr and Christian Pacifism.* A *Concern* Reprint from article in *The Mennonite Quarterly Review,* Vol. XXIX, April, 1955.

——————, *Peace Without Eschatology?* A *Concern* Reprint, 1961.

——————, *The Pacifism of Karl Barth.* The Peace Church Mission, Washington, D.C.

——————, *The Christian Witness to the State.* Newton, Kansas: Faith and Life Press, 1964.

Unpublished Doctoral Dissertations

Burkholder, J. Lawrence, *The Problem of Social Responsibility from the Perspective of the Mennonite Church,* Prince-ton Theological Seminary.

Waltner, Erland, *An Analysis of the Mennonite Views on the Christian's Relation to the State in Light of the New Testament,* Eastern Baptist Theological Seminary, 1948.

Articles

Bender, Harold S., "Anabaptist-Mennonite Attitude Toward the State." *The Mennonite Encyclopedia,* Vol. IV, pp. 611-17.

——————, "Church and State in Mennonite History." *The Men-nonite Quarterly Review,* Vol. XIII (1939), pp. 83-103.

Hillerbrand, Hans J., "The Anabaptist View of the State." *The Mennonite Quarterly Review,* Vol. XXXII (1958), pp. 83-110.

Neufeld, Elmer, "Christian Responsibility in the Political Sit-uation." *The Mennonite Quarterly Review,* Vol. XXXII (1958), pp. 151-62.

Yoder, Edward, "Christianity and the State." *The Mennonite Quarterly Review,* Vol. XI (1937), pp. 171-95.

——————, "The Obligation of the Christian to the State and Community—'Render to Caesar.'" *The Mennonite Quarterly Review,* Vol. XIII (1939), pp. 104-22.

Yoder, John H., "The Otherness of the Church." *The Mennonite Quarterly Review*, Vol. XXXV (1961), pp. 286-96.

Studies and Reports

Report to United Presbyterian Church in the U.S.A. General Assembly: "Relations Between Church and State." May 1962.

Translated Works

The Complete Writings of Menno Simons. Scottdale: Herald Press, 1956. Translated from the Dutch by Leonard Verduin and edited by J. C. Wenger.

The Author

Richard C. Detweiler was born at Souderton, Pa. He graduated from Souderton High School in 1942, and worked as a newspaper reporter for one year. He then served in Civilian Public Service during World War II, in soil conservation units located near Hagerstown, Md., and at Sideling Hill, Pa. After a medical discharge from CPS due to serious illness, he recovered his health sufficiently to enter Eastern Mennonite College in 1944 and received his BA degree in 1949.

During his junior year at EMC he was ordained by the Franconia Mennonite Conference to serve as pastor of the

Perkasie, Pa., Mennonite Church. In 1963 he resigned his pastorate to enter graduate theological studies at Princeton Theological Seminary, completing his BD requirements in 1966 and earning his ThM degree in 1967.

Besides his pastoral ministry, he has served as a teacher and administrator in Mennonite schools in eastern Pennsylvania. He was teaching-principal of the Franconia Mennonite School from 1949 to 1954, and then transferred to the newly organized Christopher Dock Mennonite High School, where he was supervising principal until 1966.

In 1954 he was ordained as an associate bishop in the Franconia Mennonite Conference Eastern District. He has served on various Mennonite Church committees and is a past chairman of the Mennonite Commission for Christian Education.

Since August, 1967, he is serving as pastor of the Souderton, Pa., Mennonite Church and continuing other duties as a bishop and assistant moderator of the Franconia Conference. He is married to the former Mary Jane Rudy, of York, Pa. They have three children.